HEART, MIND, BLOOD, SKIN

poems by

K. Andrew Turner

Finishing Line Press
Georgetown, Kentucky

HEART, MIND, BLOOD, SKIN

ACKNOWLEDGMENTS

Thank you to Michaelsun Knapp for helping me with editing. Thank you to John Brantingham for believing in my work and pushing me to write more. Thank you to my mom for your support. And thank you to my Patreon supporters Stephanie Barbé Hammer, Katy Mann, Karina Dale, and Viannah Duncan; the fantastic San Gabriel Valley community; the Long Beach poets; and all the wonderful writers in my life. I appreciate all the support, love, and companionship you have all provided.

"On Loneliness" previous appeared in *LUMMOX* 2012
"Sharcas" previously appeared in *Like a Girl: Perspectives on Feminine Identity* in September 2015
"Possess" previously appeared in *Carnival Literary*, February 2016
"Our Judgment" was a semi finalist for the Luminaire Award and appeared in *The Spark*, May 2016
"Anxiety" previously appeared in *Incandescent Mind*, Issue 1, June 2016
Previous versions of "He Should Have Been My First," "Our Second," "An Open Letter To My Gym Husband," "Your Compression Shirt," "Over the Rainbow," and "Still in Mind" appeared in *Gymlationship* by Arroyo Seco Press, February 2016

Publisher: Leah Maines
Editor: Christen Kincaid
Cover Art: Karina Dale
Author Photo: Elder Zamora
Cover Design: Elizabeth Maines McCleavy

Printed in the USA on acid-free paper.
Order online: www.finishinglinepress.com
              also available on amazon.com

Author inquiries and mail orders:
Finishing Line Press
P. O. Box 1626
Georgetown, Kentucky 40324
U. S. A.

Table of Contents

Blood

Skin

HEART

He Should Have Been My First

quiet, beneath my hands—
his body. his soft sides,
blonde hairs erect at my touch.
his pebbled skin
awakened by my breath
upon his ass.

I arrived by train,
across central california,
desert and farmland,
by bus to his mustang.

this night, afraid,
our innocent limbs tangled.

I wanted more,
but I could not ask
too timid
too new to desire
unskilled
and left to admire.
I wanted
more.

Our Second

I
We decided to go out to the Alibi
    where Mr. A's friend is a bartender
in an industrial area of Pomona.
    Mr. A was running late.

When I finally saw him walk up
he looked so good.

We hugged out front—
chatted—I only thought
        of his arms
      around me
for that brief moment.

II
He ordered me a drink
and another
   and another
      and another
      and another
   with drinks for him.

He sniggered
about what others wore
   how they acted
tight barbs
   and I believed
this was a shell
    for himself
  and his insecurities.

We touched all night:
   light touches
     across his arm or shoulder
   or my side or forearm
and he might have been so nervous.

III

The bartender,
    a bear of a man
  handed us drinks
flirted with me and with Mr. A
   though he wanted us together.
Some people
      are beautiful like that. We

drank and talked
   on the patio for the air,

though we made it to the Latin Room
   for a song. He wanted to dance.
The bar here did not have
  his friend
      so we backtracked
for another drink,
   and watched dancers.

He commented
on their empty skimpy underwear
      and I laughed along with him.
He asked me who I thought was hot
   I answered no one
     caught my attention like he did
and he smiled.

IV

At closing, we finished a drink
   and I was well on my way
when the lights dimmed again.
   We danced to music
neither of us liked.

When we stopped, he went to
  talk to his friend, the bear
  and another employee, bar-back or bartender himself

told me to go somewhere else while they talked.

I backed off to the bathroom
   waiting a couple minutes.
I decided to go home
         and walked out.

I didn't mind much
   as some people would.

V
He chased me down
   moments after I stepped outside

ran after me like in the movies

he wanted me to know
   wanted me for something
      and he couldn't let me walk.

It was beautiful.
   It was fleeting.

He held me close
     hugged me
       caressed my arms
explained: that L
was trying to set Mr. A and the bear up again
   but Mr. A wasn't interested.
   He asked if I was okay.
     I was drunk
         and thirsty.

He kissed me, told me he wanted me fired
   so I could get a better job
he wanted to cuddle all night
told me to call in sick

and I wanted to
    wanted to so bad.

To keep myself
    alive:
        I had to work the next morning
even though all I wanted was to be there
sharing
        his world.

Cracked

Ghost
     ed
        out of my life
when you'd finally arrived
and I
     thought we'd go some
                        where
maybe down the aisle
or at least down the coast

and I don't know why I'm writing
this poem for you
here in my room where we were once
     naked;

you'll never read it

you read my last one
then never came back
leaving me here
     crack
         ed
      pepper
            corn split
open and waiting
to be consum
         ed.

Dating

is like searching amazon
using your best keywords
and what you want is
                    unavailable
the next best thing
did you mean?
has a missing piece
    doesn't believe the same
    as you or

has "features" you don't want
                    don't use
                    can't even imagine or

god-forbid is out of your price range
doesn't come around when you want
or comes around when you aren't home
or is always out-of-stock or

you start thinking of settling for something
    at least for now
isn't it better to have now
than wait for mail that never comes?

all this serves to remind you
that what you want
                    is out of reach
and there is nowhere else
that delivers the same

An Open Letter To My Gym Husband

Dear Gym Husband,

First, thank you for working out
the same hours I do.
Your dedication is noted—
probably not by that bottle-blonde.
I mean, she likes your body, but can't
appreciate you like I can.

Second, I'd like you—
and your worn tan shirt and black shorts—
to know you are off the market.
We are married, in case you weren't aware.
(I'm still waiting for your proposal.)
You can only make eyes at me,
and must do so to reassure me
of our tentative gymlationship.

Last, please, I'm not staring,
merely enjoying the views opportunity
has presented me.

Now, slip on this key ring,
this membership tag,
and I will see you tomorrow.

Your Compression Shirt

How I long to be
your compression shirt:
embracing
every muscular
curve of your body.
Cupping your pectorals,
running down
your abdomen,
stretched taut across your back,
gripping your thick arms,
gathered at your hips.

Greedy, I would lick the sweat
from your caramel skin
keep you cool
keep you warm
be the envy in the weight room.

Salt Lick

Swirl your tongue
upon my neck
and devour the sweet
sweat-salt,
lean
your weight
upon
my bones.

Over the Rainbow

It is easy
        to want your hand
but to take it
is to cross the chasm carved
by hands
        with familial lies

even though I've been fighting
to tell myself
          I am worthy
to build bridges
I do not

Though I am not glass
stronger than forged steel
    fragility is engrained
shaping my direction
away
      from pleasure

only now
do I want to break
and reach
        reach
for your hand
          further
than Kansas from Oz

HIV

Sit in the chair, uncomfortable,
look at the coffee pots
see the woman in pain,
the little boy who doesn't know
    why he is there

and here I am
 a gut feeling
that I needed this

from urgent care's
    cold rooms
    to keep me from getting sick
if I had been exposed.

I wait, forget how
to breathe.
            There are no meds
here. I leave with a prescription.

As I go, terrified
and anxious, I see the coffee pot,
now full of dark liquid.

Tomorrow I begin 30 days
and hope all is well.

We Met

He said
he'd been waiting
for over a year.

I finally agreed.
I wasn't afraid
just jittery and cold.

We watched TV.
He ran his hands through my hair
and I felt okay.

We kissed
more than once
and it was not good.
I should have told him
to brush his teeth
like I had done before,
though it may
have not made a difference.

I went because my friend
had a date and I wanted
    any connection
    any way to not be left behind.
I went because Mr. A
disappeared.
I went because I wanted to feel better.

Cyclobenzaprine

Half-awake to a full body
buzz, skin tingling muscles like
butter and lead
first time to relax in ages
and the sex dream!

Two hot men
both models
one a porn star,
the other presented
in his underwear
and one said to the other
"Find your own."

Though
why not share?
Wouldn't two be best
in this dream?

Incomp

i miss
     him

  miss his smile

the way he would touch me
   the sound of

his eyes upon my

miss
     how he

his stubble kiss
 and

   miss
      the way
i would

 but then
   how can I miss
what never

how
    i long for

Still in Mind

Though I haven't
   written about S in days
he is still
    just behind my ears
 whispering to me
   exactly   what
he wants
    and I only
   want
     to say
   yes

Close Your Eyes

She says
"imagine the future"
and I see his face
and my eyes tighten
and my ribs squeeze my heart.

"Miracles can happen
at any time,"
and I begin to believe her.
Laying in the imagined
lush pillowed bed
my body relaxed.

"Imagine the future stretching
out one year from now"
and he and I are kissing
and it feels so real
that I cannot
help but smile.

"Imagine 5 years"
and I see my friend's
smile, her love, acceptance
flows like a balm for my burned self
and we are still here, still alive.
I see his arm around me.
Both grin and laugh.

"10 years" she says,
prompting the vision to change
and I see them. Older.
We relax inside her house.

It hurts to want so much love
after so many years of nothing.
And I begin to believe
that miracles can happen.

MIND

Anxiety

looks like
   pocked crag
and mountain fog
like sleep
   without the sleep

without the jar
         of being
alive except
         survival
which looks like
         not surviving

shallow breath
eyes that don't see
   petrification.

I am a statue

stuck forever
holding my arms
         aloft
beseeching change
    to come   and
save me

but
   change cannot
do anything
to stone   except
wear it down more
   and more until there
is nothing
        left but
dust
   and sand
rubble ground underfoot.

Possess

Darkness, blanket
   the world   wrap me
in embrace tight   let me
sink into your depth
   forever   love like I
want love   cannot have
   my desires realized   let
the whole of your being
drown my sorrow   come
   let me take you into
my mouth   go inside
   fill me up until
I am endless you.

hope is not a word

walk dark roads
      underneath skeletal oaks
   toward something more black
than earth's bowels
     step into the embrace
  death awakens
like a dream
       but slumber brings
  no peace   death brings
no solace
     yet is an end
  of suffering, waiting
  for pain
 the anticipation of more
 and more pain
in every shadow
  inflicted by light

desire: an end
  by any means
      because hope
is not a word
  but an ugly trap

Death is a Welcome Inevitability

simple thoughts such as
could get in a car accident
would that be such a bad thing?

you understand why people take their own lives
you can sympathize with their logic

"it's selfish" it is said "a monstrous act"
but you see it differently
as a form of freedom

freedom from pain
from the constant aches
of just existing as that is too much to bear
along with everything else

freedom from debt
from the social debts you owe
to the financial crush of student loans
credit cards
rent or mortgage
imagine that gone, in an instant
and how much relief you feel just at that thought alone

freedom from anguish
from having to be so careful all the time
and still being in pain
still experiencing the awful repercussions of being born
without your asking

freedom from the crushing everyday
choices you have to make
between eating or shelter
between family or homelessness
between desperately trying to free yourself
by any other means, and nothing, nothing
saves you

freedom from everything
from any and all decisions
think   think
imagine them all gone with no effort
how the tension melts out of your body

you even think about those you'd leave behind
and, while it makes you sad,
perhaps nostalgic,
The End is still preferable
as you are nothing more than something
crushed underfoot every waking moment

it begins to make sense
why those who choose to end it
smile their last day

these thoughts these ideas
come and go
                on and off
never stick around long enough
to do much about

no, you visualize how others
could make that choice for you
and instead of cursing them as you die
you thank them
for providing you with freedom
you could never attain on your own

then you think
right before falling asleep
how accepting death
makes it easier to live
because the only consequence
you fear is more misery

First

We watched TV,
awkward on the couch.
I drove to Pasadena
on a Monday in early March.
The room was small
a shuttered window faced the street.
I had taken a shot of vodka
to relax.

My friend gave me late advice
and (surprised at her accuracy) said
I would leave soon, that it was late.
I was bored
and wanted it over.
I moved through the action
distant, as uninvolved as I could be.

Blood rushed to my limbs.
I remember glancing to the distant
gray wall, and thinking
how ordinary this was,
how plain. A waste of time,
but for the simple
experience—hoping the next
might be better.
The most lackluster debut
one could have
into the Secrets of Adulthood.

Vertigo

Soft turn
       waves
like rolling
   eternally down hills
turning
       turning
             over
the mind
       repeating
half
   quarter
         rotations

or like being
tossed in
     Hawai'ian riptides
tearing you under
   tumbling on sand rock bottom

though you are stationary
haven't moved in days
wishing spin's end

In Vases

Daffodils in cobalt vases
awash in color

     I follow
waves
   to the ocean front
gray boardwalk
set aside the dinghy

     instead
let me wander
   sand hills
in search of spots

  of green
with sunlight in their tips
soft susurrus
     enveloping
salt air succor for burned lungs
the golden trumpet
  relief for
     tired eyes

On Loneliness

Solitude—peaceful and soothing
restoration of the soul.

Under trees,
soft laps of liquid
against stone
wood and plant

revealed in moments
around dry landscape.
Hoarse cry of toad
insistent birds looking for mates.

Sunlight splashes across
the shadow of my hand
reflecting my nature
upon nature.

Distant rush of traffic
on gentle breeze.
Faraway laughter
in spring.

Brown, gold, green
tapestry-woven over lumps
and crags
and stuffed into gullies.

I've found the burial ground
of Egypt here.
Snakes instead of mummies.

Twisted trees beseech sky
for rain, yet weeds
tell of recent showers.

I can breathe

these moments needed
never sought only given.

Thought

Under sun
       light

   wait

   watch

hope
   rain
      comes

   you wish
to drown
   in your own
        tears

Stone

Wake
   jagged rock
see water
   touch shore
let it
   wash away
your dirt
   leave you
cleansed
   flesh cold
and hard
   ready to face
anything
   watch all break
on your new
       flesh.

Speak

learn to
       speak

let yourself
          believe
  learn how
to

         help yourself
be
  find your own

voice

speak speak speak
           truth

       because
it is death
     burial

your words
   show you

you are
     worthy

Granted

wish
upon
stars

sparks
soar
from
heaven

wishes
are
never
answered
how
expected

better
worse
doesn't
matter

wishes
need
fulfillment
but
better
than
hoped

change
lives
for
the
better

they
know
more

trust
them

nothingness

nothingness stalks
   to be
fed energy
   life
   feelings

it swallows me
whole days
   weeks

   powerless
to stop its insatiable appetite.

nothingness lurks
   around every corner
and toys
   with every feeling
lets me know I am never alone

every moment happiness breaks free
   sunshine blinding
how long until
         i am swallowed

inescapable negativity
has been my companion
  for years
have i become
   exactly like it

Sunsets: As Violence

Orange stains like faded fights
smearing the sky
with remembered past assaults.
Red bleeds down
teething mountains—
like those that have teethed on us.
Cloud-gauze keep the vaults alive
long enough to heal
to wound again.
And deep purples
bruise the sky
a lovely violent shade,
in every waking moment.

Every day the ritual is repeated.
The blue afternoon
our only face
that says, "I am okay."

We are not.

We lie to ourselves
to our friends,
relatives, strangers,
like the sky lies to us.

In the dark,
the night is our false hope.
Lights so dim, so distant
they cannot be possible,
falsely warm us
with their cold gaze
and by their luminescence we wish
to guide ourselves toward
a better future.

But in the morning we are here,

purpled and battered,
our truth written in the heavens.

BLOOD

Abuse Feels Like

It's horrifying to say "I was abused"
    like some kind of drug
    or addiction like I
    wasn't human.

It's hard to admit
    see the words
    speak the truth.

I "betray my abusers
    I need to keep it in
    I am the one to blame."

My skin curdles
    thinking about it.
    "I am lying"
    "I am making it up"
    "It's in my head."

Abuse is word-bludgeon
    muscle knots
    I can't escape.
    I tiptoe not to wake the beast
    because I am never right.

I want to be small enough
    but I am
    too much human
    too much space.

It is wrong
    but feels natural, just
    like forgiving because
    he knew no better
    like wishing he could have been
    the perfect Dad
    like wishing for the perfect family

but knowing
they razed you.

I am not important enough
    I am less-than
    everyone is more-than
    and I can't stop
    can't stop forgetting myself.

Recovery is further off
    an eternal layover
    broken dishes
    after a long day
    like forgetting to pay
    my bills
    and I will
    never be home
    as nothing has meaning.

Then I learned
    understood
    I, child-parent.
    They were wrong about so much
    it takes years of convincing
    I have WORTH.
    I become myself
    like my peers began at 15
    and continued at 20
    but here I am past 30
    dis-functioning
    and still, I cannot blame.

They should have done better.

I remember
    the deliberate cuts
    from yesterday

but recreate my past
build truth from deception's detritus
until the nightmares fades
and struggling becomes
existing and morphs
into living.

Tended to by friends
I gained strength
and toiled to create
on my bruised foundations.

Grandpa's Ghost

One expects a ghost after a death:
some apparition with baleful gaze
but he is a haunting of the brain:
a prickling of the back of the neck
as if being watched;
a pinching of the third eye.

In hushed night
I walk by him standing
in his sick room, his deathbed still.
I make my midnight snack,
and he sits in his chair looking
for something he can no longer find.

Up the stairs,
his office feels crowded,
my hairs on end.
He stares at his desk, dead eyes
plead: *I cannot breathe here.*
I whisper, "You are dead."

Remembered words sting and cut sharp
even though he is no longer alive,
no longer here to tear us down.

I shut my bedroom door.
I no longer sense
his energy traversing the rooms
he occupied, searching for life
panicked about breath
he no longer needs.

wait to be free

waiting for a time
when I can finally be free
of all of them

free to do whatever
free to expand
   beyond bonzai shape

like I once bloomed
for two glorious years
when I lived nine hundred miles away
in a desert town
before I got sucked back
before I knew better
and now
        I wait to be free

Drinking With Dad

Starts with a call, Dinner?
Yes. Sounds good. Short ride over
to the treed yard.
Gravel crunches underfoot as I pass through.

Chicken in hand, tortillas, spices.
Tacos that will take three hours. We start cooking
fowl in a pressurized pot.
We each take a beer, back when we could both drink them.

His hair is graying, patches turned white.
We drink and drink
talking of the world.
Another beer? Yes, me too.

We talk more. I'm sorry he says, about that,
pointing to my room where he'd once desecrated white walls
with black marker. JESUS HATES FAGS.
I say I love him.

We speak about my mother.
He tells me another reason for them to have divorced.
Dark secrets about his cousin and her boyfriend.
How he did drugs that one night, and tested martial boundaries.
I was not surprised.

She knows, he tells me. He doesn't say much else
except for a thank you. I've acted as confessor, letting him burden me.
As he has done since I was old enough to listen.
As others lay burdens upon me.

More beer, bathroom break.
Turn off the cooker, burner, set it to cool
we rest in the outdoor breeze
glass bottles in hand, his tongue slices the air.

We go in. He grates cheese while talking

about my stepmother. How he loves her
how she drives him crazy.

I cut lettuce and tomato and avocado
barely aware of what I'm doing.
My hands and lips are numb. I do not cut myself;
I do not bleed. I stumble, but do not fall.

Unsaid: the chasm that grew almost ten years ago.
He wishes I weren't gay. I wish he didn't care about that.
He wishes I were him. I wish he were better.

Beans in the microwave, hot
tortillas next, overdone. We fill our plates
after eating olives.
I barely taste the food.

Sunscreen, sun lotion, sun tan oil

all smell tropical.
Required to prevent "lobster,"
to endure more than a moment outside
especially for the palest of us.
Like high school marching band.

We marked time for hours those sunscreen summers.
Once, it hit 120° and was humid,
the water of the grass evaporated
to help us sweat off our sunscreen—
white on our noses, shoulders, arms, legs
but never feet.

We played music late in August.
Metals and plastics exposed
in the cut grass—
we guzzled the precious liquid
(iced if you were smart)—
unbearably hot during short water breaks.

If there was shade, and time,
sunscreen would be reapplied,
changed like a dressing for a wound,
with a simple "Would you mind?" or
"May I borrow?"

At home, I showered off
grass and sweat and sunscreen—
occasionally chlorine if I had swam
in tepid water—
finally cooled enough to sleep.

Incense

Fragrant smoke twists
and curls
rising from its once-heat
to blanket the room
in energy and peace.

Outside the refuge, old used-to
fills the air: White Diamonds,
vacuum, dust, old memories,
regret, broken childhood dreams—
they all flood back,
never forgotten,
waiting for the moment
incense leaves.

Shackled to the past,
escape is only temporary—
exactly how it was wished
exactly why you wish it would
break forever.

I Am Walking

I call her once, maybe twice a week,
and I ask about her day,
tell her "I am walking somewhere."

When I was younger, she bought me
plastic calling cards, surrounded by laminated
blue cardboard, or refilled the one I had
back in the days of 10-10-220.
I talked to her, or my brother, for hours
called from California or airports
on my way across the country to visit.

Some days it felt like I grew up
in jet planes and airports.
Graduating slowly from steward care,
where I would follow the nice ladies
to an enclosed room with other children.
As a teen, I scoffed at being an "unaccompanied minor."
I grew up between Gates A202 and G-4
through O'Hare's rainbow underground.
I watched matchstick trees and play cars
grow. I watched the landscape of brown
become rolling hills of green, old trees.
She always waited for me, and smiled.

I tell her my troubles
with my dad, and she sighs,
"Yes, I know. I was married to him."
When I came out, "I love you."
She also says that I had no chance
at sanity—and we laugh.
We both know we are more sane
than most in the family.

I wish I could see her more,
now that I'm older. Wish we could
spend time together.

She is older too. I know we may lose
each other. But there are languid summer days
in the sun and powerful late-night thunderstorms,
memories of trees, bark blinding white in the sun,
pine needles blanketing earth,
and the crystalline lake on hot days
to hold me when I need to see her.

My Brother's Wedding

Watching my brother marry
    changed me
the first gay wedding
I had been to
    I had hoped,
      mine might have been the first.

He came up the aisle
stiff-legged, grining
and so, so nervous.
His groom, an emotional
mirror.

It was beautiful
    and I cried
to watch them.
    Finally
    I could relate to words
spoken and sentiments
    something
I realized I wanted again:

love.

Someone to make me smile
    comfort my fears
and love me
    and the flaws
      I know
are mountains.

Something I've wanted and
    never
      let myself
believe   I could have.

And I know

I can have
love,
   marriage,
      the whole
happy ending—all
   of it.

I have
   to believe;
have to work for it
and be willing
   to fight to keep it.

Only then will I be ready.

His Magnum Opus

I

Children are the product of those
before them and
I am no exception
no matter how hard I try.

II

My father's father abused him
physically,
emotionally,
as he was taught
as a child—
beaten into submission
by country men
with nothing better to do
than abuse a child
for amusement,
perhaps as had been done to them.

III

Nothing excuses abuse,
even past abuse.

IV

My father abused me
emotionally
his words cut
to my heart-quick
left me
to believe I was less-than
his anger
my defeat.

V

He doesn't know how he affected me.

He doesn't know that no matter how

hard he tried,
he abused me
in a different way
than his father abused him

and that is to be pitied
he tried so hard
to do better

and he failed.
Failed to protect me
from abuse by others
in our family.

I have to believe
he was as clueless as I
too terrible the consequences
otherwise.

VI
Living with his father
I know how he was treated
how his father
treated me
treated my grandmother
how we had to tread
around his mental illness
and pretend
we were okay.

VII
Our family is dysfunctional
obviously
yet we never discuss
how bad
how in pain
we truly are.

VIII

My mother suffered
though I do not know
to what extent
and yet she has learned
she has overcome her worst
in perhaps ways that let her
be a better parent to me
than she could have been years ago
when she was exhausted
and only trying to survive.

I know I have issues
with abandonment
being left alone
on my own
with nothing to fall back on
much like being left
as a child
to my own devices
often left hungry
because I learned
crying meant nothing
that nothing would garner me attention.

I forgive her.

IX

I am learning to forgive him
learning that it is for me.

I need to let go
let myself bear
the weight of emotions
tell myself
that it was not okay
no matter what

that I need to be angry
push myself to pity him
because I was the best he could do.

X
Reconcile my past
let go
learn to be free
from the chains
and write myself
as something new
and become my own
magnum opus.

SKIN

Final Day at Zeli's

A couple watches the street
drinks something dairy and sugary
   cuddling on uncomfortable chairs.

People stare at the pastry case
   looking for a reason to splurge on their waistline
 because they had a rough week.

The menu, with the prices under flimsy paper
for a year
        the printed, laminated menu
with the current prices.

Italian inspired walls
   like a villa in Rome or Greece
 with columns support the lips
   and bar that separates baristas
from us
   the writers
       and the general populace.

There is a burlap covered
chair or table and we discuss
   but come to no conclusion
on the nature of it
   though it looks more like a drum
or a vase.

The building across the street
   is finally finished
 brought to a close
and ready on the outside.

laughter

morning
laughter
like rain
gentle
and soaking
in parched desert
to cleanse
the soul
from the manacles
of depression
anxiety
and C-PTSD

friends in
coffee shops
are balms
for the wounded
the healing
crutches
so we can
learn to walk
on our own
but never alone.

Untitled Poem

poems
sometimes
refuse
to come
out
on the page
instead
they sit
on tips
of lips
fingers
toes
or points
of ball pens

poems
evade
napkin
capture
or steno
notepads
computer
screens
minds
or voice

poems
play
and giggle
as they
escape
again
laughing
like sprites
stumble
over
ethereal

forms

poems
age
sometimes
let
themselves
be captured
when ready
even if
they wait
a lifetime
too long.

Stained Glass

Let sunlight
           filtered
through
   windows
      that have seen
dirty rain
   and snowfall
know they're
   strong as the light
that streams in
unbroken stained glass

beautiful
       historied
fragile
     full of life

some are broken

know their stories
    their light.

Writing Group

Coffee shop writing
happens so little
we talk
drink coffee
gossip
tell stories.

We bend to keys
think of something else
to say, speak
   and laugh
mourn, sympathize.

We are characters
in each other's lives
   in our own
and we gather together
to write
even if we create
in our own minds.

Our gathering is writing:
spoken words
gestures, actions
all in a setting so popular
so cliché.

Our Judgment

Sit
down
look across the room
table
cups of coffee
stains of past
cups of coffee
or tea or water
or beer or wine
and
watch:
the woman
in a straw hat
read yesterday's
last month's
newspaper
then leave
with her shopping
basket;
or the man
drop his backpack
then read
a paperback
like he doesn't
want to be home
with his
perhaps-wife
and maybe-kids;
or the girl
playing with her
dolls blond
and white
unlike her;
or the couple
in ugly sweaters
for christmas
walking arm in arm

like they were
happy;
or the woman
in leggings
like she'd come
from yoga
or the laundry mat;
or the young man
staring
at her leggings
because he feels
he can
birth-gift-right
of being man;
or the woman
in pink
with a backpack
kawaii
with maybe-kids
and a yes-husband
who is judged
to be too old
for a kawaii
backpack;
or the cars
driving by
parading;
or the screen
blocking
construction from view;
or the homeless
near-invisible
with their yes-hungry
stares and
yes-sad eyes
and their yes-needing
pleas

and our no-I-cannot
smiles;
or boys
on skateboards;
or girls
on skateboards;
or birds
in the trees
or on the ground
or eating;
or the benches
we sit in;
or everyone
or the clouds
or nature
or anything
watch
with our
senses
alight
the world
judged in
every word.

Do Not Be Him

Tall, strange man
in a beige trench coat
working, maybe,
who analyzes handwriting
—free for beautiful women
charges for "ugly"—
what a charming
misogynist
who loves free money
and playing games.

He is a poem,
a story,
waiting to be told
as a warning:
Do not be him.

Friend's Cafe

Antiqued blue table
with burlap sack planter
a tropical plant's leaves
protect

       benches and chairs
emblazoned with the logo
and *Friend's Cafe*
fill the otherwise empty floor
but we sit in comfy chairs
with brick floor—a fireplace
should be here with us.

Shiny flower art lines the wall
80s music on the stereo
as the workers chat behind
the register
Tiffany lamps warm the room
inviting openness

yet employees are trapped
in a small space,
hopefully because it is
easier to reach and grab quickly
though it still resembles a cage.

July 6, 2015

Muted sunlight, hazy shadows,
play on the ficus berry-stained
sidewalks

       empty chairs and tables
green and brown
symbols of the large
environment eerily
devoid of usual crowds.

Three men sit across for me
one with blondwhite hair
and a red Hawaiian shirt
too young to wear
something so dated,
a thin, darked-haired man
in a black shirt,
and a man with blue-green eyes
who borrowed money from his friends

there is a dog fight in the crosswalk
though cars only wish to hurry
down the Avenue
off to somewhere else no matter
the time of day
ignoring safety rules
and speed limits

there were poets behind me
discussing lines and reading aloud
and one voice sounded familiar
but I didn't know her face.

Finally, families show up
under these yellow banners
and umbrella shades
while the American flags

dance in the breeze
just after the nation's birthday celebration.

Pictured, Christmas

Tree is burdened with tinsel
and cheap baubles.
An empty azure bowl
that once held candies
or cashews
rests precisely on a doily.

Two eager boys, dressed in tuxedos—
one in a white jacket, one in black—
meet the old man's eyes.

The girl in a blue dress with sheer shoulders
stands demure,
yet her lip curves down in defiance
of her father—
his rigid posture looming,
back turned to the camera.

The boy in the white jacket
holds her hand
yet their fingers are hidden
by the corsage she wears.

Her sister stands in white,
hands clasped in front of her
gaze on the floor, as if chastised.

Perhaps the couple waits for permission.
Perhaps they never had it,
nor never will.
It does not matter to them.

But she doesn't love him
like she thinks she does
or like she hopes she does.
She loves him as rebellion.

And he can't care
to see past her fervent desire,
only knowing the now
not her mutable future.

The Age of Gemini Begins

two strangers
grasp hands
one hand extended
towards the other
rough skin embraced

at the lip of a well
meeting for the first time
one hand reaches
to grasp another
under the westering sun

each knows the other
through sign
but the tongue
they speak
tells a geography
different than
the one they are in

as a reflection
communication
remains scrambled
nothing more than noise
that separates them
the skies they know
only twilit in between

lush greens
and vibrant blues
of the ocean
backdrops of mountains
purple in the setting sun

trees at meadow's edge
cut brilliant sky
waves crashing on shore
rise up like knives
gold in morning's light

the other from lands
rich in rivers
covering miles
hues of green
vast and unimaginable

far to the south
wide and strong jungles
cut by silver ribbons
trees and ferns wild
within its embrace

here
at the lip of a well
they grasp hands
and say everything
with their faces
their bodies
and trade foods and stones

in some middle
where dust settles
once again
with no words
they say their peace
mirrored and friendly
telling stories

it is a beginning
of something
beautiful
and terrible

an end
wondrous and pure
in every way
portents of future inevitable

Sharcas

Grandpa calls me a silly girl
when I watch the sun set.
I love the vibrant hues,
the transformation
from orange
                        to red
                                    and purple
the painted vaults of the sky.

I watch the Gods lower the sun
and leech the vivid color
into homogenous, inky black.
Only pinpricks of light
that we call sharcas—
wandering flames.
I wish to wander with them,
dance in the velvet blanket,
but Grandpa calls me silly.

I am supposed to be strong
support our village
            by feeding them
            protecting them
I am told I should be
like my brother.

But all I want to do
is gaze into the ether
and leave these chains behind
and soar with the sharcas
forever free
forever free
no longer a silly girl
but a woman
burning bright
shedding hope
in eternal darkness.

K. Andrew Turner writes in prose and poetic forms and his works span the lyrical, literary, and speculative genres through a queer lens. While his fictional works explores human relationships through the mundane or absurd, his poetry focuses on introspection through self, mental illness, and observations of others. Through the process of therapy, his writing has become not only unchained, but also deeper and reflective.

He teaches and mentors writers among the palms trees and under the eternally sunny-skies of Los Angeles via traditional approaches and with meditative techniques to help his clients evolve and re-define their work. He has taught workshops throughout Southern California to various writing groups. In 2013, he founded East Jasmine Review—an electronic literary journal—where he remains as Publisher and helps guide the focus of the magazine to help diverse voices reach audiences.

Arroyo Seco Press published *Gymlationship*, his first chapbook, in 2016. K. Andrew Turner's work has also appeared in *Chiron Review, LUMMOX, Carnival Literary, Sadie Girl Press, MUSE* and other magazines and anthologies. He was a semi-finalist for the 2016 Luminaire Award for poetry. You can find more about him and his work at: www.kandrewturner.com. Follow him on twitter @kandrewturner.

www.ingramcontent.com/pod-product-compliance
Lightning Source LLC
Chambersburg PA
CBHW021155090426
42740CB00008B/1097